Little Italy

The Story of London's Italian Quarter

Tudor Allen

First published by Camden Local Studies and Archives Centre

Drawings by Rachel Dilworth
Layout by Mark Aston
Printed by WCS Digital Print, 27 Mount Pleasant, London WC1X 0AS

Camden Local Studies and Archives Centre
Holborn Library
32-38 Theobalds Road
London WC1X 8PA

www.camden.gov.uk/localstudies
E-mail: localstudies@camden.gov.uk

ISBN: 978 1 900846 21 9

Acknowledgements

The author would like to thank the following for their kind permission to reproduce photographs in this publication: O. Comitti and Son Ltd, Islington Local History Centre, St Peter's Italian Church, Victoria and Albert Museum (photograph by Paul Martin, p.29), Joseph Gazzano, Brian Girling and Eileen Nichols.

All other illustrations have been supplied by Camden Local Studies and Archives Centre. Every effort has been made to trace copyright holders. Apologies in advance to those concerned if an oversight has occurred; corrections will be included in any future editions of the publication.

Front cover and title page illustration:
Eyre Street Hill looking north around 1900

Contents

Italian boys in Little Saffron Hill around 1900

Stranded on a Foreign Shore

> *"Most persons are aware that there is an Italian colony at Saffron Hill, but it is strange how few visitors ever penetrate this curious quarter. The Italians have certainly succeeded in keeping themselves apart from the rest of the population. Whole courts and alleys are entirely inhabited by these foreigners; there is not a single English person among them."*
>
> Adolphe Smith in *Street Life in London* (1877)

In 1875 Joseph Greenwood wrote, "The unaccustomed wanderer has altogether lost sight of his native land, and is stranded on a foreign shore." The place he was describing was London's Italian quarter. Italians had been living in London for many years prior to 1800 but they were few in number and widely scattered across the capital. However, during the 19th Century, there grew to be such a concentration of Italians within part of the Holborn area of London that the locality became known as 'Little Italy'. This book takes a look at the fascinating history of this community from its origins in the early 1800s up to its last years in the late 20th Century.

Little Italy is hard to define geographically and it has been said that for its inhabitants it was more a way of life. However, roughly speaking, the Italian quarter was situated to the north and south of where Clerkenwell Road lies today. To the north of Clerkenwell Road it was roughly bounded on the west by Rosebery Avenue and on the east by Farringdon Road. To the south it occupied the streets around Saffron Hill, Leather Lane and Hatton Garden. For the most part, it was a maze of narrow, overcrowded streets, alleys and courtyards. Although the English christened the area 'Little Italy', among the Italians themselves it was known as 'The Hill', after Back Hill, one of its principal streets.

The First Settlers

> *"Some of these artisans earn from twenty to thirty-five shillings a week."*
>
> Count E. Armfelt in *Living London* (1903)

In the early 19th Century Italian craftsmen began to settle in the Holborn area of London. These skilled workmen came from the northern part of Italy, mainly from the regions of Piedmont and Lombardy, many from the Alpine valleys near Lake Como. They were principally makers of looking glasses, picture frames and precision instruments such as barometers and thermometers. Why did they come to England? Probably because of the political situation in their own region of Italy and the economic effects it was having on them. The Italian craftsmen would have been attracted to Holborn because of its location close to the City and the West End and because it was an established centre of craftsmanship.

They set up business in its wealthier commercial streets – streets like Hatton Garden and Charles Street (or Greville Street, as it was later known). They often lived in large houses which contained both their workshops and their homes and were comparatively affluent.

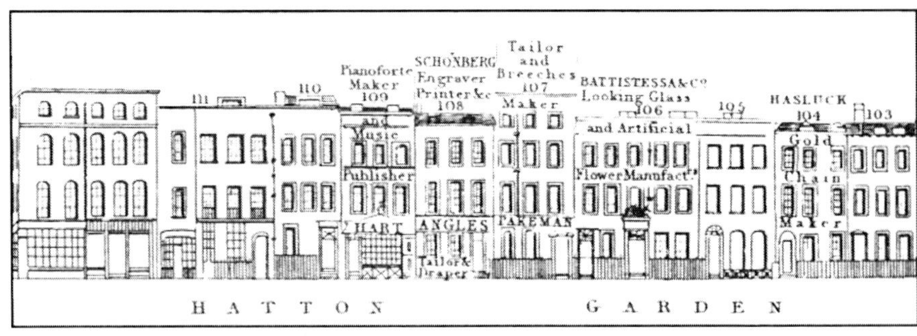

Section of Hatton Garden from *London Street Views* by John Tallis (1838-1840).
No. 106 is occupied by an Italian looking glass maker

Hatton Garden around 1908. Looking north from Holborn Circus

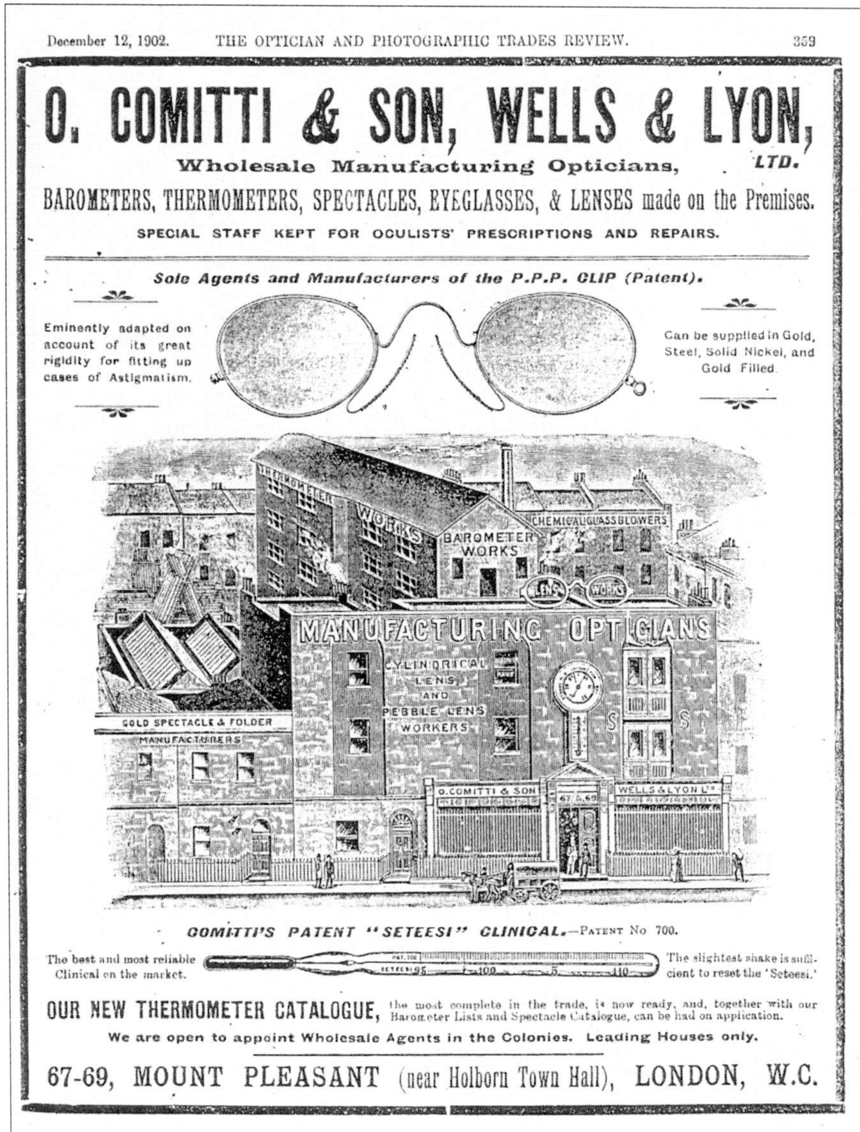

Advertisement for O. Comitti & Son from 1902

Famous Firms

One of the most highly skilled crafts practised by the Italians was the making of precision instruments such as thermometers and barometers. Enrico Negretti, from Como in North Italy, was a thermometer maker and glassblower in Leather Lane. Joseph Zambra, born in London of Italian parents was another Holborn-based glassblower. In 1850 the two men joined forces and set up a precision instrument making business in Hatton Garden called Negretti and Zambra. Before long it had established an international reputation for the excellence of its products and was able to advertise itself as:

> *"Optical and Meteorological Providers to HRH Queen Victoria, the Royal Observatory and the British Admiralty."*

The company was particularly famous for its barometers but, over the years, made a range of other items including thermometers, cameras, telescopes and optical and aircraft instruments. It continued to operate up until 1981 when it was taken over by Western Scientific.

Another celebrated Italian barometer maker – O. Comitti and Son – was also based in Little Italy, at 67-69 Mount Pleasant. The firm, nowadays based in Ongar in Essex, maintains its international reputation for fine quality barometers and clocks.

A skilled craft of a different kind practised in Little Italy was organ making. As we shall see, one of the main occupations of the Holborn Italians was organ-grinding and many of the barrel organs were made by the firm, Chiappa and Sons. This business was established by Giuseppe Chiappa in 1877 at 6 Little Bath Street (later known as 31 Eyre Street Hill). When organ-grinding declined in popularity, Chiappa and Sons moved into the production and repair of organs for fairgrounds and bioscope shows. These were particularly popular in this country in the 1920s and 1930s. The business continues to this day and is still based in its original premises.

Ice cream seller in Caroline Place in Little Italy around 1890

The Rookery

By the mid 19th Century the Italian craftsmen who had first settled in the Holborn area were far outnumbered by a second wave of immigrants from Italy. They were poor and unskilled, driven to seek work abroad by the poor economic conditions in Italy which had followed the Napoleonic Wars. Most of those who came to London made their way there, principally by foot. Initially the majority originated from the north of Italy, from the foothills of the Alps in Lombardy and Piedmont or from the central regions of Italy, from Emilia and Toscana. Later on, however, southern Italians came to Little Italy in greater numbers, many coming from the Liri Valley region between Rome and Naples.

At this time the streets around Saffron Hill and Leather Lane included one of London's worst slum areas. Houses were in disrepair and therefore rents were low and many of the poor Italian immigrants settled here. There was great overcrowding and Saffron Hill was known as 'The Rookery' because of its crowded tenements. In 1879, in Eyre Street Hill, inspectors from *The Lancet* medical journal found a house which contained as many as fifty people. Conditions in Little Italy were also insanitary. *The Lancet* inspectors in 1879 found, in Somers Court:

> *"...the drains so constantly stopped that they over flowed and the inhabitants had to place planks on stones so as to step from house to house without treading in sewage matter lying exposed in the open court."*

Surveys in the 1880s found that conditions in Italian households were the worst in any group. It was feared that these poor living conditions would lead to the spread of epidemics and these health concerns led to much slum clearance in the Little Italy area in the late 19th Century. The area where the Italians settled also had a reputation for crime. Field Lane - situated where the southern part of Saffron Hill is today - was notorious for pickpockets and dealers in stolen goods and it was no accident that Dickens chose this street as the location for the thieves' den in *Oliver Twist*.

Wagner and Monkeys

In 1851 a third of the working population of Little Italy were travelling street musicians. By 1871, this had risen to almost half. While some played instruments such as hurdy-gurdies, harps and fiddles, most played mechanical barrel organs. These came in a number of varieties including piano organs, hand organs, good quality 'opera' organs and comic 'jig' organs. Some of the organ-grinders had monkeys, trained to climb up balconies, dance, beg for money, salute and thank. The music the organ-grinders played could be quite adventurous. According to Adolphe Smith in 1877:

> *"The Italian organ-man has actually ventured to render extracts from Tannhauser and Lohengrin to the startled inhabitants of our crowded thoroughfares."*

Many of the organ-grinders came from the Parma region in central Italy. Others came from Naples. Within Little Italy, they tended to live close together. In 1871, for instance, sixty-one organ grinders from Bardi near Parma in Emilia were living in three houses in Summers Street and Little Saffron Hill. Similarly, forty-six Neapolitan organ-grinders were living in adjacent houses in Summers Street, Fleet Row and Eyre Place.

Summer was the lucrative time for the street musician and many were seasonal migrants who returned to Italy in the winter. Nevertheless, most organ-grinders earned less than a general labourer.

Organ-grinders at the junction of Eyre Street Hill and Warner Street, as depicted in *The Graphic* in 1875

Organ-grinder with hand organ in London around 1885

Deliberately Out of Tune

Not everyone was fond of the Italian organ-grinders. By the middle and professional classes they were regarded as something of a nuisance. It was said that many of the organ-grinders deliberately played out of tune to "extract money in return for silence on their departure." The magazine *Punch* launched a campaign against them. In 1864, a law was passed to curb street music.

The law had little effect. However, by the late 19th Century, organ-grinding was in decline and ice cream selling had become the favourite occupation of the Holborn Italians.

The street music tradition in Little Italy evidently continued, nevertheless, well into the 20th Century. Recalling her childhood in Holborn, an elderly lady in the 1970s wrote:

> *"My grandfather was particularly famous in the Hill, as he and Mr Enrico Votrona used to go from house to house on Christmas Eve welcoming the coming birth of the Saviour with traditional Italian tunes. Mr Voltrona played a flute and my grandfather played a type of bagpipe instrument called a 'zampogna'. Their visit was eagerly awaited in the households of the Hill as, to many, it marked the real beginning of the Christmas celebrations."*

Hot Codlins

While all the organ-grinders of Little Italy have long since passed into obscurity, there was one Italian entertainer from the locality, however, who achieved immortality. His name was Joseph Grimaldi. Born in 1778, Grimaldi was the son of an early Italian settler in the Holborn area where he is said to have grown up. At the age of three he made his debut at Sadler's Wells theatre in Finsbury. It was the beginning of a stage career that was to last almost fifty years. The comedian performed mainly at Sadler's Wells and in Drury Lane Theatre in Covent Garden. He is regarded as the founder of modern clowning and became so popular that the name 'Joey' has passed into the English language to mean clown. Between 1818 and 1828 he lived on the fringes of the Little Italy area in a house in Exmouth Market which still stands today. He died in 1837.

Grimaldi's most popular song was *Hot Codlins* about an old lady who sold roast apples or codlins as they were once called.

> *"A little old woman her living she got*
> *By selling codlins hot, hot, hot.*
>
> *And this little old woman who codlins sold*
> *Tho her codlins were not, she felt herself cold.*
>
> *So to keep herself warm she thought it no sin*
> *To fetch herself a quartern of ..."*

At this point the audience would supply the final rhyming word - "gin" – for which Grimaldi would reprimand them with the words "Oh! For Shame!"

Joseph Grimaldi as the clown in *Harlequin and Friar Bacon*, as engraved by Robert Cruickshank around 1820

Little Italy ice cream seller in 1877

Hokey-pokey Men

> *"The sale of ice-creams was unknown in the streets until last summer and was first introduced by a man who purchased his ices of a confectioner in Holborn... The buyers had but a confused notion how the ice was to be swallowed."*
>
> Henry Mayhew in *London Labour and the London Poor* (1851)

One of the most common occupations of the Italians of Little Italy was ice cream selling. Penny ices sold in the streets became a craze during the later 19th Century. By 1900 ice cream vending had replaced organ-grinding as the most popular job of the Holborn Italians. At that time there were around nine hundred ice cream sellers living in the area, many in Saffron Hill and Summers Street. They would get up early in the morning to mix and freeze their ice cream and then set off with their carts or barrows to sell it around London. They were so many in number that, according to Adolphe Smith writing in 1877, when they set out with their barrows "it is a veritable exodus. The quarter, at first so noisy and full of bustle, is soon deserted."

Originally the ice cream was not served in cones or wafers but in little glasses called 'licking glasses'. This was not very sanitary. The customer would lick the ice cream off the dish and return it to the vendor who would rinse it, then fill it for the next customer. The ice cream became known as 'hokey-pokey', and the Italian ice cream sellers as 'hokey-pokey men'. It is thought that this derived from the cry of the seller in Italian of "ecco un poco" (here is a little piece) or, "o che poco" (oh, how little), referring to the cheap price.

An Artistic Sight

The ice cream sellers would make and decorate their barrows themselves. Some barrows were decorated with pictures of Italian royalty, and even of English royalty. Doubtless Queen Victoria graced one or two! According to Count E. Armfelt, writing in 1903, the barrows could look quite splendid:

> *"Below, in the back-yard, there may be seen gorgeous paintings freshly varnished – they are the outside covers of the ice-cream barrow. And, when put together, when the snowy-white top is furnished with its shining brass fittings, the Italian ice-cream barrow becomes an artistic sight."*

Most of the Italian ice cream sellers came from the south of Italy, many from the region of Calabria. They were compared favourably with the English poor for the discipline they displayed in their working lives. Armfelt wrote: "the Italian iceman sets an example of steady perseverance, economy and foresight which is at once the envy and the marvel of the English poor who live around." Many reputedly carried two purses – a visible one containing only a few coppers, and one, secreted about their person, which was full of gold! Certainly, ice cream selling could be lucrative and many of the vendors were able to afford a cottage and plot of land in Italy to enjoy in their old age.

Little Italy ice cream seller in 1903

Gatti and Bolla's Café-restaurant depicted in1899

Penny Ices

In the ice cream trade, small family businesses were the norm, but, in a few instances, they developed into large enterprises - none larger than that of Carlo Gatti. A Swiss-Italian, Gatti arrived in London in 1847 aged thirty and virtually penniless. He started out with a stall selling coffee, goffre (a kind of waffle), roast potatoes and roast chestnuts. Then, in 1849, he joined forces with Battista Bolla, a chocolatier from Castro in south-east Italy, to establish a café-restaurant called Gatti and Bolla. This was located at the southern end of Little Italy at 129 Holborn Hill on the corner of Leather Lane close to Holborn Circus. Gatti and Bolla also lived there with their families. Here they sold drinking chocolate, a novelty at the time. According to an obituary of Gatti, in 1849 he made a trip to Paris from where:

> *"He immediately returned with a machine for manufacturing chocolate. The machine was an old and rusty one, but that was all he could get with the money at his disposal. He and Battista Bolla set themselves to place it in working order and began the manufacture of chocolate before the very eyes of the public at the house numbered 129 Holborn Hill..."*

In 1853 Gatti started selling ice cream. Before long, his penny ices had become a Victorian craze. As his business grew, Gatti built a wharf by the Regent's Canal where he stored, in two huge wells, ice imported from Norway. The ice was transported by ship to the London Docks, then by barge along the canal. The building today houses the London Canal Museum. The ice stored there was sold to a variety of customers for refrigeration and in this way Gatti pioneered the refrigeration revolution in the food industry. Later, in the 1860s, Gatti opened a palace of varieties in Westminster Bridge Road and a music hall in Villiers Street off the Strand. Though much altered, the music hall still stands today, home to the New Players Theatre. When he died in 1878, Gatti was reputedly a millionaire. His was truly a rags to riches story.

Fortune Telling

On the shady side are the women and girls on stools and chairs knitting and sewing... while in the courts and alleys, where no one intrudes, girls are washing and ironing and cooking al fresco in true Italian fashion."

Count E. Armfelt in *Living London* (1903)

Initially there were few Italian women in the Little Italy community, as most of the Italians were single young men only temporarily in the country. However, as the Italian colony became more established, Italian wives and daughters became more numerous.

The women of Little Italy did a variety of work. Some were domestic servants. Others manufactured pasta. They might make lace for wealthy ladies, for altar cloths or for the vestments of priests. Many did laundry work, washing and drying it in public wash-houses, then ironing it back in their homes. Among the customers of the washerwomen were Italian waiters working in the catering business in Soho.

Some women made money singing, dancing and playing the tambourine, although, according to Charles Booth in 1902, "many of the so-called Italian girls are Irish dressed up in Italian clothes."

An interesting occupation engaged in by Italian women was fortune telling by means of love-birds or parakeets. According to *Wonderful London* edited by St John Adcock in 1927:

> *"The old Italian woman goes about with a folding stand and a parakeet in a cage. The bird is possessed with great powers of discrimination. In its cage are a number of cards. So soon as someone has been persuaded to test their fortune, the parakeet has a look at the customer, selects the card which it considers most appropriate, and pushes it through the bars."*

Little Italy fortune teller in 1903

Little Italy boy harpist in 1877

A Traffic in Children

> *"A traffic in children has grown into a regular business. We are told that a band of villains, an association of modern slave-traders, purchase helpless children in the neighbourhood of Naples, promising to teach them how to play or sing. In the meanwhile they are most cruelly treated."*
>
> Adolphe Smith in *Street Life in London* (1877)

Many of the children of the Italian quarter worked on the streets of London. Some were street musicians, playing accordions, hand organs, concertinas and other instruments. Others collected money for organ-grinders. Some sold plaster statuettes or roast chestnuts. Then there were those poor children who, sadly, were forced to beg.

These children often worked for masters called 'padroni' who had brought them over from Italy. Most of the children employed by the padroni came from southern Italy, usually walking all the way to their new homes in Holborn. Often they were leased to their masters by impoverished parents. In some cases, they were even kidnapped. Once in London, many were treated cruelly. Their working day could last from nine in the morning up to eleven at night. Their earnings went to the padroni who, reportedly, were often able to afford to retire to Italy after a few years, thanks to the money made by these poor children.

This child exploitation was widely opposed. Giuseppe Mazzini, the Pallotine Fathers, the Charity Organisation Society and the Italian Benevolent Society all worked against it. The Italian Relief Society rescued many children and sent them back to Italy. Thankfully, the passing of the Children Protection Act in 1889 helped combat this trade in Italian children and it was gradually suppressed.

Some Other Occupations

As well as the kinds of work already mentioned, a number of other occupations were common among the Italians of Little Italy. For instance, during the 1850s many men came to Holborn from Italy who were makers and sellers of plaster statuettes, both sacred and secular. In 1861 as many as a fifth of the workforce were engaged in this occupation. They principally came from a few villages in the mountains near Lucca in Tuscany. In this region of Italy, there is a long tradition of figure-making and one of the towns in the area – Coreglia Antelminelli – today has a museum dedicated to this craft.

In the 1870s Italian knife-grinders began to settle in Holborn. They came from a few villages in a valley called the Val Rendena in the Italian Dolomites in north-east Italy. These men moved from place to place pushing a cart whose wheel was also used to sharpen knives. According to James Strang in 1899:

> *"The best earnings are made by the knife-grinders, who perambulate with a wheel. These are looked up to as a rather superior class."*

Another occupation engaged in by some Italians – in fact at one time they had a virtual monopoly over this kind of work - was the making of mosaics and terrazzo, for instance for the floors of public buildings. The mosaic workers mainly came from a few villages in Friuli in north-east Italy and began settling in Little Italy in the 1870s.

Many Italians worked as asphalters, surfacing new roads with asphalt. This was tough work and according to Charles Booth in his 1903 *Life and Labour of the People in London*:

> *"The English man apparently cannot be induced to undertake this work, alleging, no doubt truthfully, that the heat brings the skin off his feet."*

Many Italians also sold roast chestnuts, imported from the mountain valleys of Italy.

Knife-grinder in London around 1892

LITTLE
ITALY
Mount Pleasant
Avenue
Great Bath St.
Warner St.
Rosebery
Eyre
Laystall St.
CLERKENWELL
Portpool Lane
GRAY'S INN ROAD
Brooke St.
THE SABINI GANG
MAZZINI
GARIBALDI

L. TERRONI & SONS
SPECIALITA
FOREIGN WINES & PROVISION IMPORTERS
CAFE RESTAURANT
NEGRETTI
RINGDON ROAD
SAFFRON HILL
Street
Kirby Street
Hatton Garden
Ely Place
Wall
Hill
RN

Leisure Italian Style

> *"If it is a fine sunny day you will see the men sitting on the doorsteps or along the walls, their knees closely bent against their stomachs in Oriental fashion, smoking curved reed pipes, and nursing their limbs with folded hands."*
>
> Count E. Armfelt in *Living London* (1903)

Little Italy at its height was like a village centred around its church – St Peter's Italian church in Clerkenwell Road. It had its own pubs, cafes, grocers, schools, clubs, even its own shoe-shine boy. There was very much an Italian flavour. The Italian language was widely spoken – most of the Italians when they arrived in England could not speak English and would have found it difficult to learn as they were, for the most part, illiterate. Furthermore, the Italians brought with them Italian leisure pursuits such as the hand game of morra and the tarantella dance. The key event of the year was the annual religious procession through the streets of Little Italy in honour of the Madonna.

Organ-grinders' kitchen in Saffron Hill depicted in *The Graphic* in 1875

Dancing in the Street

Dancing was popular in the Italian community. Sometimes the Southern Italian dance, the tarantella, would be danced in the street, accompanied by castanets and tambourines.

Little Italy also had a number of dancing saloons. In 1903 Count E. Armfelt describes how:

> *"One of theses saloons is in a cellar which is reached through a narrow court. The cellar gives hardly any light and previous to an entertainment a big fire is lighted to counteract the damp which issues from the ground and the walls. The furniture consists of a few pictures, a small improvised bar, and two dozen rush-bottomed chairs. The only musical instrument is an organette with a handle to it, and every dancer as a rule gives a 'tune'."*

Two women dancing the tarantella in Little Italy in 1903

A Taste of Italy

Italians set up food shops in Little Italy catering for the Italian community and supplying Italian provisions such as wine, pasta and olive oil. For instance, in 1890, Luigi Terroni, an Italian from Pontremoli in Tuscany opened a food shop in Clerkenwell Road, close to the Italian church. The store continued to run, in its original premises, until as recently as 2007, when, sadly, it closed its doors for the last time. Up until the 1980s, it was still run by the Terroni family itself.

Terroni's around 1900

In 1901, Alfredo Mariani opened an Italian provisions store in Farringdon Road. In 1944 the store was taken over by his son-in-law, Giuseppe Gazzano, and in 1954 became known as Gazzano's. The store is still in business to this day on the same site in Farringdon Road and, with the closure of Terroni's, is now the oldest surviving Italian food store in the locality. The current proprietor is Joseph Gazzano, Alfredo Mariani's grandson.

Bessie Mariani around 1914 inside Mariani's, the food store started by her husband

A class at St Peter's School as depicted in *The Graphic* in 1875

St Peter's School

As the Italian community became more settled it formed its own institutions – Italian schools, clubs, an Italian hospital and an Italian church.

In 1842 a Catholic school for Italians opened in Little Italy in Leicester Place, Saffron Hill, founded by Father Angelo Baldacconi and known as the Italian Catholic Free School. When the school was later taken over by the Pallotine Fathers who ran the Italian church of St Peter's, it became known as St Peter's School.

The location of the school changed several times. For a short period it was even based in the crypt of the church. In 1878 it moved into its last location in Herbal Hill.

The staff included teachers who were Italian so that children with little English could be taught in Italian. Many of the teachers and pupils were Irish as there were large numbers of Irish immigrants living in the Little Italy vicinity. At its peak, around 1900, St Peter's School had as many as three thousand pupils.

In 1953 the school became known as St Catherine Labore. Seven years later, the secondary school closed but the primary school continued to occupy the same premises until the early 1980s. Today the building is home to the Central Ballet School.

A Nest of Young Conspirators

The first Italian school in Little Italy was the Free School for Workers which opened in 1841. It was founded by the famous Italian patriot Giuseppe Mazzini, one of the key figures in the achievement of the modern united state of Italy. It started at 5 Hatton Garden where there is today a commemorative plaque to Mazzini. Later, it moved to nearby 5 Greville Street.

When he founded the school, Mazzini was living in London, in exile from his native Italy and with a death sentence on his head. His school provided free education for the children of Italian workers as well as for destitute child workers whose exploitation by cruel masters was of great concern to Mazzini. On weekday evenings boys were taught reading, writing, mathematics and elementary science at the school. On Sunday afternoons they were taught drawing and Italian history.

Mazzini himself taught at the school. One English observer said of the boys' attitude to Mazzini, that they "revered him as a god and loved him as a father". Other teachers at the school included the pioneering otologist, Joseph Toynbee, and the Italian poet and scholar, Gabriel Rossetti, father of the poets Dante Gabriel and Christina Rossetti. For many years the director of the school was the celebrated 'improvisatore', Signor Pistrucci, who used to improvise rhymes on subjects suggested by his audience. Charles Dickens was a generous benefactor of the school.

Not everyone approved of the school. One Italian clergyman organised demonstrations against it. A more orthodox Catholic school in Sardinia Street near Lincoln's Inn Fields was suspicious of the liberal and anti-religious instruction it believed the school imparted. On one occasion a mob from Sardinia Street reputedly marched to the rival school intent on vandalising it. The famous historian Thomas Carlyle called the school "a nest of young conspirators." At any rate, the school was short-lived. By 1861 it was down to a mere twelve pupils and before long closed.

Giuseppe Mazzini around 1860.
Mazzini was once described by the great 19th-century thinker, John Stuart Mill, as "the most eminent conspirator and revolutionist now in Europe"

Members of the Society for the Progress of the Italian Working Classes in London, 1914

The Mazzini Garibaldi Club

"Have faith in the immortal cause of liberty and humanity. The history of the Italian working classes is a history of virtue and national glory."

Giuseppe Garibaldi in a letter to the society in 1864

"Affection, advice and assistance, all this you shall have from me until death. Your cause is my cause, your faith is my faith."

Giuseppe Mazzini in a letter to the society in 1864

In 1864 a working men's club was opened in Little Italy, a mutual assistance society for the men of the community. The club was called the Society for the Progress of the Italian Working Classes in London, later becoming known as the Mazzini Garibaldi Club.

The club was co-founded by two of the key contributors to the achievement of the modern united state of Italy – Giuseppe Mazzini, who spent much of his life agitating for a united Italy, free from foreign domination, and Giuseppe Garibaldi, who in 1860 conquered the Kingdom of the Two Sicilies. The club was founded a short time after Garibaldi's triumphal visit to England in 1864. Mazzini himself framed its first constitution and was its first president.

The club was originally located at 106 Farringdon Road. Later it moved to 10 Laystall Street where there is today a commemorative plaque to Mazzini. In 1933 it moved into its last home in Red Lion Street just a few streets to the west of the Little Italy area. In its heyday the club formed the heart of social activity for the men of the Italian quarter. During World War II it was requisitioned as enemy property and closed down. It reopened in 1951 but, sadly, closed its doors for good in 2008.

A Hospital for Italians

Giovanni Ortelli was a London Italian who had become wealthy through importing cheese into the city. Conscious of the number of Italians in London and the difficulties they often experienced in hospitals through their lack of knowledge of English, Ortelli decided to open an Italian hospital.

There was a real necessity for such a hospital as, by then, there were so many Italians living in London. The site chosen for the hospital was Queen Square in Bloomsbury. It was no accident that this was close to the large concentration of Italians in Holborn.

The Italian Hospital opened in 1884. Most of its medical staff were Italian speaking. As many of London's Italians were poor, the hospital provided free health care to Italians and anyone of Italian descent. It also provided treatment for people of other nationalities. In 1898 it was rebuilt on the same site, again by Ortelli.

Annual balls were held to raise funds for the hospital. These were major occasions in the Italian community's social calendar.

During World War II, the hospital was damaged by bombing and closed and then subsequently requisitioned as enemy property. It reopened in 1950 but during the 1980s the spread of Italians to other parts of London reduced the demand for treatment at the hospital to such an extent that debts forced its closure in 1989.

The building still survives, though, and today is part of Great Ormond Street Hospital.

The stucco-fronted main façade of the Italian Hospital

The interior of the Italian Church as depicted in an 1863 edition of *The Illustrated London News*, shortly after its opening

A Huge Cathedral to St Peter

St Vincent Palloti was an Italian priest who in 1835 had founded in Rome, a religious congregation called the Pallotine Fathers or the Society of the Catholic Apostolate. In the early 1840s the first member of this Society, Father Raffaele Melia, became co-chaplain to the Sardinian Chapel at Lincoln's Inn Fields, just a little to the South of Little Italy, with responsibility for its Italian worshippers. Around 1845 Palloti and Melia conceived the idea of a church for London's Italians. Funds were raised for the church in Italy and other European countries and a site was chosen in Holborn because of the number of Italians living there. The idea of the Italian church was however strongly opposed, as, at the time, there was still a lot of hostility to the Catholic Church in England. For instance, in a debate in the House of Lords, the Bishop of London commented:

> *"In this country Catholics can take advantage as they please of places to celebrate their faith, but apparently this is not enough for them. On the contrary, although they know full well that they have ample places of worship, they have submitted a proposal to build a huge cathedral to St Peter in this city, whose metropolitan cathedral is dedicated to St Paul."*

Vincent Palloti did indeed have hopes that the church would promote Catholicism, writing: "In converting this country to the true faith we would in effect be converting those innumerable populations over whom it reigns or over whom its army as good as gives it power."

However, despite the opposition, the building of the church went ahead and, on 16th April 1863, the Italian Church of St Peter's was dedicated by Cardinal Wiseman, the Cardinal Archbishop of Westminster. It was a grand ceremony, attended by eleven bishops and over fifty priests including, among others, Augustinians, Benedictines, Capuchins and Dominicans. A full orchestra played Haydn's *No. 3 Mass*.

A Church for All Nations

The church was of central importance to Holborn's Italian community, the centre of the Little Italy 'village'. More than that, it was and still is at the heart of the Italian community in London. However, though dedicated as the Italian Church of St Peter, it has always been intended as a church for all nations and over the years it has attracted Catholics from many countries besides Italy. It has always been run by the religious congregation founded by St Vincent Palloti – the Pallotine Fathers.

St Peter's was the first Italian church outside Italy and, when it opened, the only church in this country in the Early Christian Roman Basilica style, its interior almost an exact replica of San Cristoforo, a church in Rome. It was also the largest Catholic church in the country until the opening of Westminster Cathedral in 1903, and would have been considerably larger had enough funds been raised to enable it to be built as originally planned. Its bell, organ and decoration were also notable. Weighing three and a half tonnes, the bell was, for a period, the largest in any Catholic church in England. The original organ, at the time of its installation in 1880, was regarded as the finest in the country. In the mid-1880s the interior was lavishly decorated with paintings and frescoes made by two Italian artists from Piedmont in northern Italy, and the Catholic journal, *The Tablet*, in May 1886 anticipated that:

> *"The interior of the Italian church will be one of the finest examples of ecclesiastical decoration in Great Britain."*

Music has played an important role in the history of the church. From 1863 until 1910 Rossini's *Stabat Mater* was performed there every first Sunday of the month. Italian musicians have often played at the masses and given concerts of religious music. The famous Enrico Caruso on one occasion sang on the steps outside the church while another great Italian tenor, Beniamino Gigli, sang at High Mass in the church in October 1949.

The Italian Church around 1918

The altar of the Italian Church

Gunfire in the Church

In the late 19th Century Polish Catholics in London had for a period no church of their own at which to worship and for a while were permitted to have mass in the Italian church. In January 1880 a shocking event took place in the church during a Polish service. The Catholic periodical, *The Tablet*, reported it as follows:

> *"On Saturday 10th January, St Peter's Italian Church was the scene of an appalling outrage. During the course of a mass celebrated by Fr James Bakanowski, immediately after the beginning of the Creed, a pistol was fired at him from within the Church. The bullet buried itself in the altar. The altar server rushed immediately into the sacristy, closing the door behind him, preventing the priest from getting in. The assailant fired two more shots at Fr Bakanowski, missing him. The priest sought to take refuge behind the altar, pursued by the would-be assassin, and succeeded in making his escape while the gunman aimed two more shots at him... Witnessing this assault, the congregation were at first too terrified to move, but after a few seconds some of them surrounded the gunman, disarmed him of the pistol and the hatchet he was carrying, and soon afterwards marched him off to Clerkenwell police court."*

It transpired that the assailant was an Italian road layer called Schloss from Saffron Hill. He was found guilty of premeditated murder and sentenced to life imprisonment. No motive was ever established for the attack.

The Wrong Man

> *"The man with a moustache is the man that did it."*

The shooting in the church is not the only dramatic crime to have taken place in Little Italy.

On Boxing Day 1864, a fight broke out between some English men and a group of Italians in the bagatelle room of The Golden Anchor public house in Saffron Hill. During the incident, one man was fatally stabbed.

The chief suspect was a local Italian glass silverer called Serafino Pelizzioni. He was brought to the bedside of the dying man who identified him as his assailant, with the words, "The man with a moustache is the man that did it."

Pelizzioni was charged with the murder and stood trial at the Old Bailey. Though vehemently protesting his innocence, he was found guilty and condemned to death.

Meanwhile, however, Enrico Negretti, co-founder of the famous firm Negretti and Zambra, and a highly respected member of the Holborn Italian community, was taking an interest in the case. He had become convinced that Pelizzioni was, in fact, innocent and that the true culprit was the accused's cousin, a picture frame maker called Gregorio Mogni who closely resembled him in appearance.

Negretti tracked Mogni down and obtained a confession from him. Subsequently Mogni was convicted of manslaughter and Pelizzioni was reprieved.

Woman standing outside the City Arms Public House in Little Saffron Hill around 1910

Members of the Sabini gang around 1920.
Seated is Enrico Cortesi. To the right, wearing a cap,
is Darby Sabini and centre-back is Harryboy Sabini.

Organised Crime

During the 1920s and 1930s the leaders of London's underworld were the Sabini brothers, gangsters who hailed from Little Italy. Their gang was known as 'The Italian Mob'.

The gang leader was Charles Sabini, known as Darby. He ran a protection racket, extorting money from race track bookies as well as from other criminals. The gang leader, Colleoni, who appears in Graham Greene's novel *Brighton Rock*, is said to be based on Darby Sabini.

Originally, Sabini's gang included the four Cortesi brothers – 'The Frenchies' as they were known – who also came from Little Italy. But in 1922 the Sabinis and the Cortesis fell out when the Cortesis requested a larger share of the gang's profits.

On 19th November 1922 gang warfare came to Little Italy when the Cortesis attacked the Sabinis in the Fratellanza Club in Great Bath Street. Harryboy Sabini was shot and injured while Darby was punched, hit with bottles and had his false teeth broken!

According to *The Times* report of the subsequent trial:

> *"The Cortesi said that the Sabini were the worst people in the Italian colony, and the Sabini retorted that there was a good deal to be said against the Cortesi."*

In Honour of the Madonna

In July 1883 an important event took place in Little Italy. A procession was held in honour of the Madonna of Mount Carmel. It is said that this was the first Catholic procession in England for some 350 years; the first public Catholic event in the country since the Reformation. The procession became an annual event, the highlight of the year for Holborn's Italians. Since 1896 only in wartime has it not taken place. It is held on the feast day of the Madonna of Mount Carmel – 16th July – or the first Sunday after. The event is organised by the Italian Church. Starting at the church, the procession snakes through the streets of the former Little Italy, which are closed to traffic for the occasion. Crowds flock to watch the spectacle pass by – the statues, the decorative floats, the band, the regional costumes, the biblical scenes. Afterwards there is a celebration or, as the Italians call it, a 'sagra'. These days this is held in Warner Street, with stalls selling Italian food, drink and other goods.

Decorative float at the procession in the 1950s

Scene from the 1933 procession

Crowds at the procession in the early 1900s

Genius for Decoration

Although the procession is still a great spectacle, it is true to say that it is not the event it was in the heyday of Little Italy when it was a much bigger occasion, the highlight of three days of celebrations. Then it was much more of an event for the local people. Just as villages back in Italy would have their own celebrations of their local saints' days so the Italian community of Holborn had its own 'festa'. On the evening before the procession a band would play late into the night. At the procession itself, not just the pavements, but the windows, roofs and balconies, would be packed with spectators. Statues, votive lights, flowers and candles filled the windows of the houses – altars to the Madonna. Decorations would transform the streets of the locality: Describing the procession in 1903, Count E. Armfelt wrote:

> *"Little Italy displays all its artistic genius for decoration. Imposing triumphal arches are erected at the entrances of the streets, garlands of flowers span the roadways, flags wave high and low, coloured lamps reach from house to house, gay tapestries hide the dilapidated walls, the street-corners are ornamented by large illuminated frames which bear the statue of the Madonna, and even the narrow courts and alleys blaze with flowers and brilliant coloured lights."*

After the procession the crowds would converge on Saffron Hill where friends and relatives would greet each other. Little Italy took on a carnival atmosphere with singing and dancing to the accompaniment of accordions and barrel organs. The street party would continue well into the early hours.

The End of the Story

In 1937 John Sperni from Little Italy achieved the distinction of becoming mayor of the borough of St Pancras. Within a few years he had been interned. World War II was indeed a difficult period for Holborn's Italian community. Following Mussolini's declaration of war against Great Britain in June 1940, many Italian men from the locality were imprisoned and Italian institutions like the Italian Hospital and the Mazzini Garibaldi club requisitioned as enemy property. While Sperni had been under observation by the police as a committed fascist supporter of Mussolini, many of the Italians interned felt they were imprisoned unjustly. Furthermore, many Holborn Italians lost loved ones when in July 1940 the Arandora Star, a ship taking Italian men to internment in Canada, was torpedoed by the Germans with the loss of close to five hundred lives. On top of this, the streets of Little Italy were heavily bombed.

Little Italy no longer exists today. Although many of the old street names still remain, slum clearance, road building, property development and wartime bombing have vastly altered the look of the area. By the early 1950s much of the original housing had been pulled down. Few Italians live in the locality today. They have gradually moved to other parts of London, often as they have become better off. Many, for instance, moved to Soho where a second 'Little Italy' developed. As the Italians have moved away, Italian businesses and institutions have folded. For instance, both the Italian Hospital and St Catherine Labore school closed in the 1980s, while, within the last year, the Mazzini Garibaldi club and Terroni's food store have both come to an end.

Saffron Hill in April 1941 shortly after an air raid

The Spirit Lives On

Yet even today some echoes of Little Italy's former glory still remain. On Farringdon Road Gazzano's still provide an enticing array of Italian food and drink, as it has done since 1901. In Eyre Street Hill no. 31 still bears the sign of Chiappa and inside the firm continues in business, as it has done here since 1877. On Clerkenwell Road, the beautiful church of St Peter's still remains, still as ever the focal point for the Italian community in London. What is more, every July there begins and ends at the church the century-old tradition of the Procession of the Madonna of Mount Carmel, when Italians from London and further afield come together and keep alive the spirit of London's Little Italy.

Joseph Gazzano, current proprietor of Gazzano's,
inside his delicatessen in Farringdon Road